AFRICAN MYTHOLOGY

SANDRA GIDDENS AND OWEN GIDDENS

The Rosen Publishing Group, Inc., New York

To Justine and Kyle with love and appreciation

Published in 2006 by The Rosen Publishing Group, Inc.
29 East 21st Street, New York, NY 10010

First Edition

Library of Congress Cataloging-in-Publication Data

Giddens, Sandra.
African mythology/Sandra Giddens and Owen Giddens.—1st ed.
    p. cm.—(Mythology around the world)
Includes bibliographical references and index.
ISBN 1-4042-0768-6 (lib. bdg.)
1. Mythology, African.
I. Giddens, Owen. II. Title. III. Series.

BL2400.G5 2005
299.6'113—dc22

                                                              2005014591

Manufactured in the United States of America

On the cover: A Nigerian screen depicting a male and female couple beneath the sun, the moon, and a rainbow.

CONTENTS

INTRODUCTION

The tsunami that struck Asia in December 2004 took hundreds of thousands of lives. Through extensive media coverage, we have the scientific explanation of how the tsunami formed. We have reports of the effects on people and property, and information about the worldwide response to the disaster. When tsunamis occurred thousands of years ago, people had fewer resources at hand to explain the seemingly angry wave. Nevertheless, they tried to answer the question of how a tidal wave could instantly, without warning, destroy so many lives. The explanation that resulted was often in the form of a myth.

What is a myth? A myth is a traditional story that has its roots in ancient folk beliefs. It usually attempts to interpret natural events, explaining the culture's view of the universe and the nature of humanity.

Every culture has its own mythology, which was designed to help people understand the phenomena that influence their daily lives. Globally, there are common themes and symbols between different mythologies, even between civilizations that have had no direct contact with each other. Some of the most common myths are the ones dealing with the creation of the universe. Others deal with heroes, gods, the origins of human beings, as well as death, the afterlife, and the change of seasons. There are myths dealing with the origin of evil, floods, the sun, the moon, heaven, hell, and even tsunamis. Myths also cover important human values like courage and bravery.

Myths across all cultures have served the singular purpose of providing answers to that which is difficult to explain. Shown here is a grieving woman after the 2004 tsunami, which struck Southeast Asia and reached as far as the eastern coast of Africa. At least 200,000 people perished in the natural disaster, which affected a dozen countries. Myths attempt to explain our relationship with nature.

Why are there similar myths from around the world? There are two main theories that try to answer this question: the diffusion theory and the parallel origin theory. The diffusion theory states that through travel, trade, conquest, and other forms of human contact, myths have been dispersed throughout the world. The parallel origin theory maintains that people in different areas of the world developed similar myths because the basic ideas behind all myths are the same. All humans are born and die. We experience a life of joy and pain; observe night and day; wonder about the sun, moon, and stars; and share the earth with other living creatures.

Whichever theory is correct, the reality is that myths exist in almost every culture around the world. Looking at these myths and understanding their themes and messages may give us some insight into our heritage and an understanding of our present-day culture.

1 THE ROLE OF MYTH IN AFRICAN CULTURE

We know that humankind was born in Africa millions of years ago, but we do not know how these first people thought. It is very difficult to date African mythology, but we do have the cave pictures of the San bushmen. Some of this rock art depicting myths of that time has been calculated to be more than 30,000 years old. African tribes feel that their myths have helped them survive the uncertainties of life. These same myths arise from ancient wisdom born long before modern civilizations. The myths of Africa, passed on orally, may give us a glimpse into the past and help us understand the modern culture.

The mythologies of Greece and many other cultures are drawn from vast literatures, based on oral stories, which were written down and preserved through the centuries. To enjoy the myths or to see how they evolved, one just has

Shown here is a gourd fashioned into a container by the San, a people who have a rich mythological tradition.

to read them. But in the study of African mythology, a great obstacle is met at once: there are no ancient books. There are innumerable stories, but these were not written down until more modern times. The art of writing was unknown in the tropical forests of Africa. This was mostly due to isolation from other world cultures. From the eleventh century AD, Muslim missionaries brought their writings to many African people along the Nile River, but neither the religion nor the writing penetrated the forests and spread to the rest of the continent. In other parts of Africa, myths were passed down orally from generation to generation and rarely written down.

Since there were few ancient written collections of myths in Africa, Europeans and Americans decided to put the African oral stories to paper. As a result, when these collections were finally written down, a number of these age-old myths were influenced by

Members of the San, also known as bushmen, are shown here hunting on a savanna in Namibia, a country on Africa's southwestern coast. The San, or Saan (singular "saa"), are a native people of southwestern Africa, namely the countries of Botswana, Namibia, and southeastern Angola. This San painting *(inset)* depicts figures who are likely hunting.

African mythology, much like mythologies of all cultures, has been influenced by outside societies, cultures, and religions. Though Islam never had a great influence on the mythology of Africa, the Muslim religion was present. Shown here is a twelfth-century Muslim map that shows Egypt surrounded by the Mediterranean and crossed by the Nile. This is the area where Muslim missionaries brought their writings in the eleventh century.

these other cultures' teachings, interpretations, and philosophies. African myths were shared and in many places continue to be shared through ritual storytelling, which was the way the African people passed on their traditions and beliefs from one generation to another.

About Africa

Africa is very large. In fact, it is the second-largest continent in the world. It is 11.7 million square miles (30.3 million square kilometers), three times larger than Europe and 23 percent of the total landmass of Earth. Yet it contains only about 9 percent of the total world population—fewer than 770 million people—but who speak more than 1,000 languages.

The Mediterranean Sea lies to the north, separating Africa from Europe. The Red Sea is in the northeast, separating Africa from Asia. The Indian Ocean is to the east of Africa, and the Atlantic Ocean is to the west. African peoples and cultures have survived in very difficult geographical conditions. A lot of the land is made up of wild deserts and jungles. The Sahara is among the largest of the deserts and covers more than 3.5 million square miles (9 million sq km). It is considered to be a vast, inhospitable ocean of sand. The west side of Africa is composed of grassy plains, the savannah, that stretch from Gambia and Senegal in the west across to Kenya in the east and down to South Africa. The central part of Africa (Uganda, Democratic Republic of Congo, Republic of the Congo, Gabon, and Cameroon) has tropical forests where trees grow to 100 feet (30 meters) or more. In many areas the primeval forests have been cut or burned, but there is still an impressive part of the ancient forest left today.

There are many exquisite but dangerous animals thriving in Africa. Africans have developed a keen respect for all living things and the land itself. That respect is embedded in their myths, which contain key elements to understanding the cultures, customs, and

Africa is a continent with a vast diversity of wildlife, and these surroundings have greatly influenced the mythology of its peoples. A large percentage of African myths involve this wildlife. The trickster myths are about animal figures overcoming seemingly insurmountable odds by the use of their wit and cunning.

beliefs of African peoples. Although people may see Africa as a single entity, it is very much like Europe in that it is made up of many separate countries, each having its own identity with its own traditions and history. Africa is not one culture but a mixture of peoples and tribes. The people who have settled in forests are in small communities, sometimes fewer than 100 to a village. There are still nomadic tribes, following their old traditions and keeping alive their old beliefs and myths. Africa also contains many large cities. There are, in fact, several dozen cities with more than 1 million people living in them.

The African Slave Trade

To understand the present, one needs to consider the past. A horrendous part of Africa's past is the slave trade. When Africans were shipped to other countries as slaves, they brought their myths with them. Long before the slave trade took place from Africa to America, Arab traders shipped African slaves to India, Indonesia, Egypt, Turkey, and Persia. Then, from the sixteenth to the nineteenth centuries, as many as 14 million enslaved Africans were shipped from the west coast of Africa to the Americas. Those who survived the deadly Atlantic crossing were bought and sold like cattle and forced to spend the rest of their lives in slave labor to white owners. Throughout these tragedies, slaves tried to keep their languages, cultures, and myths alive. Most slave owners tried to stifle traditional practices, but many slaves met secretly to retain their heritage and myths.

Shown here is a photograph of an African slave in the Belgian Congo. The African slave trade took place along the west coast of Africa. European slave traders built trading posts from Senegal to Cameroon and traded rum, cloth, guns, and other merchandise for slaves, whom they brought back to the Americas.

Religion in Africa

Africans are very religious people. This was not apparent to missionaries or early explorers, who perceived the Africans as barbarians with beliefs different from their own. Religion pervades most aspects of the African cultures. In the southern lands, Christianity has become dominant, and the north is primarily Muslim. In tropical Africa, traditional religions are alive and still practiced. Traditional religions are closely linked to local cultures. They play an important part in helping people understand natural events like weather, harvest, or childbirth. Many Africans blend elements of both traditional and other religions together.

One of the best-known African religions is vodun, or voodoo. Some of the slaves who ended up in Haiti came from the West African Fon and Yoruba territories, and some came from the Congo. The name vodun derives from the Fon word for god, *vodun*. In West Africa, people believed in deities who controlled the weather and held prime positions in the Fon religion. Since the slaves were forced to practice their religion in secret, an aura of mystery surrounded their rituals. To the Africans, voodoo symbolized their active resistance to oppression and provided a religious bond to their native homeland. But the slave owners looked at voodoo as dark and evil. The wooden figures that Fon people used to communicate with their deities were banned by slave owners who regarded them as idols. The Africans made smaller ones out of cloth so they could hide them. This is the origin of the voodoo doll.

African myths are not merely lighthearted stories for children, nor are they simply unscientific explanations of the universe. While much of African mythology is religious in nature, not all myths are necessarily religious. Myths express ancient beliefs that justify social institutions and established customs and values. There are different kinds of myths. Some deal with activities like hunting or fishing, and some deal with social order, laws, customs, values, and ideas. And there are those that deal with creation. As we'll see in the coming chapters, the mythology of this vast continent addresses a wide variety of themes, which helped the African peoples cope with the numerous uncertainties of life.

2 THE CREATION MYTHS

From earliest times, people everywhere have tried to understand the origins of the world they live in, the origins of the human race, and the natural forces surrounding them. The most common myths in African cultures are creation myths. The creation myths of Africa are as varied as the many cultures that inhabit the continent. Creation myths play an important role in African societies as they set the framework for the social, political, anthropological, and economic structure of the society.

African creation myths do not deal with why the universe exists. There is no attempt to look beyond the existence of the world. One unique feature of many African myths is that although Africans lived in isolated pockets without means of

This stone statuette was the communicator between the Kissi people and the creator god.

communication with other people, their myths have many similar themes and ideas. African creation myths explain why God, who once lived close to humankind, has removed himself from their world. Most of these myths describe a golden age when there was no separation between humans and their creator.

Many African people living apart from one another throughout the continent tell the following myth of how the sky and Earth became separated. In most of these myths, something occurs that alienates the people from their god. The Mende people say that God withdrew into the heavens because humans continually begged for benefits and favors from him, as in the following myth.

The great creator god lived very close to his people, just a little above their heads in the sky. The people would take the creator god for granted. The women would reach up to the sky and take a little bit of blue heaven to add to their soups, and the children would scramble among the clouds, cleaning their greasy hands off on them after eating a meal. The women used long pestles to pound their cereals in a deep mortar carved from a log, and when they were energetic, these pestles would protrude into the sky and sometimes even hit the creator god. One day the creator god got hit by the pestle in his eye, and he rose up in a fury. Both he and the sky rose up to their present position.

Another common version of the separation of Earth and sky is that there was a rope or thread that linked these two bodies and provided a means for the celestial deity to communicate with

This is a Mende woman who is wearing what is known as a Sowei costume. This costume is worn by the older women during a ceremony celebrating a girl's transition into adulthood. The mask rests on the shoulders, and the dress is made of grass.

humans. Myths from the upper White Nile area speak of the relationship between God and man being severed when the rope between heaven and earth was accidentally cut.

Many parts of Africa contain their own versions of creation myths fitted to the experiences and circumstances of the people. The Yoruba, for example, have a rich mythology, with gods and spirits who have great influence over the lives of human beings. Their myth of creation is linked to the traditions of their tribe.

Olodumare was the god of the sky and had two sons, Obatala and Oduduwa. He sent them down to earth with a bag, a hen, and a chameleon. There was no land, so the brothers had no place to stand. Their father dropped a tree from the sky, and his sons landed safely in the branches when they descended to earth.

Obatala tapped the tree and started to drink the palm wine that was inside. He soon became drunk off the wine and fell asleep. Oduduwa climbed down the tree to

The Yoruba is one of the largest groups in Nigeria. Shown here is a bottle, which is covered in beads, shells, and cloth, made by a Yoruba artisan. The Yoruba people have a great social and political diversity. Yoruban society is patriarchal, and members of the father's lineage live together and share names, taboos, deities, and lands.

These wood carvings of twin figures were created by Yorubas. In Yoruban culture, twins, whose births are unusually frequent, are a sign of good luck. The Yoruban people have one of the highest rates for twin births in the world, and it is considered a great misfortune if one or both of the twins are lost.

the roots, which were in water. He opened the bag he brought and discovered it contained sand. He quickly tossed it on the water's surface.

The chameleon walked on it, and it held his weight. Oduduwa emptied the rest of the bag, and the hen scattered the sand in all directions until the sand particles became land. Olodumare sent Aje (prosperity) from heaven as a gift and gave his son three gifts: a bag of maize to sow for food, a bag of cowrie shells to trade with, and three iron bars that he forged into knives, machetes, and hoes. Obatala eventually woke up and created beings from clay. Because he was drunk, he fashioned beings that were imperfect and handicapped.

Obatala is an important god of the Yoruba people from Nigeria. Since Obatala, under the influence of the palm wine, created crippled people, he became the patron god of the handicapped. When slave masters prohibited the mention of Yoruban mythic figures, these Africans found a Christian saint whose attributes corresponded to those of Obatala and other gods. They could then worship their traditional gods under the guise of paying homage to Christian saints.

In the Congo, a tribe from the rain forest tells a myth of creation in which Earth has been made by one god alone, Mbombo. Again, their myth is closely linked to the traditions of their own tribe.

In the beginning, there was nothing but darkness and water. All were ruled by the god Mbombo. One day, he had a terrible pain in his stomach and vomited up the sun, the moon, and the stars. There was light everywhere. The rays of the sun made some of the water turn to steam and rise up to make clouds. Dry hills emerged as the level of the water dropped. Mbombo vomited once again, and trees, then animals and people emerged. Among everything there was one trouble-maker and that was lightning. It caused so much trouble that it was eventually chased into the sky.

Creation myths in Africa are strikingly similar to those from vastly different cultures and places. A common theme of many creation myths is that the sky, Earth, the sun, the moon, the land, and the seas were all created by a superior being. Though African creation myths often vary from culture to culture, they all bear the same elements.

What is fascinating about Africa is that in some areas creation myths have similarities to the Bible's book of Genesis. The following myth is told by the Basari people as well as the Mbuti people of the Congo, told long before their encounters with Christian missionaries.

God made the first man and woman and put them in a forest. They had everything, including an abundance of food, at

their fingertips. God told them that they should have children and that all humanity would live forever. He warned them not to eat the fruit of the tahu tree. Both the man and woman agreed to what God promised. The man was never interested in the tahu fruit, but the woman, when pregnant, had a terrible craving for it.

The man stole the fruit for her, and together they peeled and ate it. They hid the peels under a pile of leaves. God created a wind and uncovered the peels beneath the leaves. God was angry that the couple had gone against their promise to him. He turned to the woman and said that women will suffer pain in the delivery of their children. God told them both that from now on they would have to work hard, suffer illness, and eventually would die.

The Mbuti people, shown here, are part of the larger Bambuti group. The Mbuti creation myth resembles the biblical story of creation. The Mbuti people live in the Ituri Forest of Zaire. This Mbuti "bark cloth" *(inset)* was made by pounding a piece of cloth and then painting it with charcoal and fruit juice.

In Africa, life and death constitute the basis for religion and philosophy. Life and death both come from the creator and are so closely linked that one cannot be conceived of without the other. Many African myths having to do with explanations of death have the common theme of sending humans two messages, one of immortality and one of mortality. The first message to reach a human will determine the person's destiny once and for all.

In many cases, God entrusts the message of immortality to a slower animal, while the faster animal bears the message of mortality. The chameleon was thought to be one of the ancient animals that created the universe. Because of its slow disposition, it was too late in bringing the message of the Great One to all people. So instead, the lizard brought death to the world, dooming every living creature to die. There are many variations of the following myth. One rendering is a Thonga myth based on this premise.

When the first human beings emerged, the chief sent two messengers. Chameleon was entrusted with this message: "Men will die, but they will rise again." Chameleon, true to his nature, walked slowly to deliver his message. On the other hand, Lizard was told to tell mankind: "You will die, and you will rot." Lizard speedily delivered the message, passing Chameleon on his way. When Chameleon finally delivered his message to mankind, they said to him, "You are too late. We have already accepted another message." This is why mankind is subject to death.

Here is another version of this myth from central Africa. It has the same theme.

When Death made his first appearance in the world, people were taken aback. They sent the chameleon to God to ask why God had sent them Death and what they should do. God gave the following message to the chameleon: "If they want the dead to revive they must throw boiled grain over the corpse." The chameleon took a long time to get back to the people.

Death continued to rage on throughout the households. The survivors needed help and could not wait for the chameleon's answer, so they chose the lizard to ask God the same question. The lizard quickly found God, but God became very annoyed at being asked the same

The chameleon was a heavily symbolic figure in African mythology and continues to be prominent across many African cultures. Shown here is a contemporary carved wooden headdress of the Afo people.

question twice. He told the lizard that the people should dig a hole in the ground and bury their dead in it.

On the way back, the lizard overtook the chameleon and delivered his message first. By the time the chameleon arrived, the dead were already buried in the ground. Therefore, because of humanity's impatience, men and women were deprived of immortality.

Variations of this myth are told in many parts of Africa. The chameleon is sometimes overtaken by a hare or a snake, but in all stories the ending is the same: the message of life arrives too late. Humankind is doomed to die.

The following is another creation myth. This one is from the Bulu people of Cameroon.

Zambe was the son of the supreme god Mebe'e, and he was responsible for creating a chimpanzee, a gorilla, an elephant, and two men, one an African and the other a European. Zambe gave all these creatures tools for survival. The tools consisted of fire, water, food, weapons, and a book. He left them with their tools, and in time he returned to see how they fared. Zambe asked each of the creatures, "All the tools you were given for survival, where are they now?" The chimpanzee had discarded everything except for the fruit.

After hearing that, Zambe banished all the creatures to the forest forever. The elephant did not remember what he did with his survival tools. The European man discarded the fire and kept the book, and the African man discarded the book and kept the fire. Thus it came to be known that Europeans remained the keepers of the books and the Africans remained keepers of the fire.

The African creation myths teach us much about how people view life and death. What we should also remember when reading them is that myths having to do with creation exist in many other parts of the world as well. Creation myths are not exclusive to Africa. So even though African cultures are unique, the subject matter of their mythologies is often as universal as life itself.

3 THE ANIMAL AND TRICKSTER MYTHS

There are many animals in Africa, from leopards, chimpanzees, and elephants to an extensive variety of birds and fish. African mythology is filled with animals, which have played a prominent role in African myths due to African people having lived in close proximity to the wild animals that shared their land.

In many African myths, people attribute human feelings and desires to animals and derive ethical behavior from the animals' actions. Some of these popular animals include the snake, the spider, the chameleon, and the antelope.

This gold weight was made in the shape of a snake by the Ashanti (also spelled Asante) people of Ghana.

The Trickster Myths

Trickster myths are myths in which an animal or insect is gifted with unusual cunning. The trickster of Bantu Africa (eastern, central, and southern Africa) and the western Sudan is the hare. In West Africa (Ghana, Liberia, and Sierra Leone), it is the spider, and in Nigeria and Benin, it is the tortoise.

Tricksters are often admired for their resourcefulness and ability to beat the odds. They have the cunning to outwit their enemies, who could otherwise destroy them. Through the trickster's mischief and frequent conflicts with the gods, the trickster becomes the source of good as well as evil in the world. In some of the trickster myths, the side effect of its lawlessness is the creation of social order.

In the oldest versions of the trickster myths, the characters are animals with magical powers. For example, the spider can climb up to heaven, the lion can devour a whole village of people, and the python can stretch from horizon to horizon. The snake was regarded as immortal because it has the real ability to shed its skin and still live. In African art, a snake depicted with its tail inside its mouth, as in a circle with no beginning or end, is considered to be the symbol of eternity.

The python is often deified, or attributed godlike powers, in African mythology. According to one myth, the snake carried God in his mouth while Earth was being created. The excrement of the snake created mountains, and because of the weight of the mountains, God feared that Earth would sink into the sea. Therefore, the snake coiled itself around Earth to sustain it. The coil could never be loosened; otherwise all of creation would collapse.

In West Africa, the spider is named Anansi and is portrayed as the most clever of the animals. It often appears in myths in which it is the chief official of God among men. It is something of a scoundrel but well liked. The spider was thought to be the one who was commanded to spin a delicate thread that reached up to God in

The snake was an important symbol in African mythology. This plaque, which decorated the palace of the Obas of Benin, is a carving of a python. Pythons were seen as symbols of strength because of their ability to transition from land to water. A snake with its tail inside its mouth forming a circle was a sign of eternity.

the sky, so people would have a path to heaven. The spider has been depicted as a great hero. It was considered to be very cunning and capable of overcoming difficult plots. One myth involving Anansi is called "How Anansi Tricked God."

Anansi, the spider, was very conceited and boasted that he was more clever than God himself. God was angry when he heard this and sent for Anansi to bring him "something." God would

*not tell Anansi what the something was, so the spider was left
to his own cunning devices.*

*He left the sky and went down to earth. He called all
the birds and took one feather from each of them. He used the
feathers to fly up into the sky and perched outside of God's
house. No one, including God, knew what kind of bird this was.*

*When the people said for God to contact Anansi to get
the answer about what kind of bird it was, God reported that
he had sent Anansi on an errand to get the sun, the moon,
and the darkness. Once Anansi overheard what God had in
mind, he now had the answer to the riddle of what the
"something" was.*

*He went to ask the python, who knew where the sun,
moon, and darkness were to be
obtained. He soon col-
lected these objects
and put them into
a bag. He then
went back to
God and
brought darkness
out of the bag. He
then drew out the*

This is a bracelet from Benin. Carved on the bracelet is a spider. In addition to being represented in African mythology as tricksters, such as in the myth of Anansi, spiders were regarded as divine in the Grassfields region of Cameroon. They represented wisdom and ancestral history.

moon. But when he took out the sun from the bag, the light was so brilliant that people who kept their eyes open were blinded.

So this is how blindness came into the world. But to the others who had shut their eyes, the sun did no harm.

All of these trickster tales are interesting because they have a moral and are comparable to myths from other cultures. They show that the Africans who generated these myths were in close contact with nature. Africans also saw the animals in these myths as having many human attributes. By portraying the animals in this way, the trickster myths gave hope to people in a society who felt oppressed or were viewed by other cultures as being weak. These trickster myths were also taken by the slaves to America. In fact the popular American retelling of *Brer Rabbit*, about the tricksterlike figure Brer Rabbit, originated in Africa. It was popularized in the United States in the stories of Joel Chandler Harris.

Animal Myths

The Igbo animal myth called "The Mermaid and the Chameleon" is told in many versions by West Africans. It is based on the story of the chameleon, the West African spirit who can change his appearance to mimic others. "The Mermaid and the Chameleon" shows not only that gods can be vain but that clothing and dress hold special places in African cultures. In Africa, clothing is a way of showing importance and wealth. How one

This is an illustration from the American version of *The Adventures of Brer Rabbit* by Joel Chandler Harris. The story, which originated as an African trickster tale, was transmitted to the New World by African slaves. Brer (or brother) Rabbit is the characteristic trickster, an oppressed figure whose intelligence and cunning allow him to outwit his animal counterparts such as Brer Fox, Brer Wolf, and Brer Bear.

dresses can say a lot about the social status of a person. In Yoruba, the kings dressed in robes and crowns made from thousands of coral beads. Gold jewelry was one of the ways people showed their wealth and importance.

Mermaid was the queen of the oceans, lakes, and seas, and felt she should be the supreme god. Chukwu was the creator and lord of all created things in heaven and on earth. Mermaid decided she would challenge Chukwu. Mermaid was regarded by all creatures, people, and gods as the most sophisticated and fashionable being of them all.

She decided to hold a contest between Chukwu and herself as to who was the best dressed. The day of the contest arrived and Mermaid put on a gorgeous dress from cloths she wove herself. Chukwu sent Chameleon to get Mermaid. Being a creature of the water, she did not know that the Chameleon was able to change appearance at will.

When she arose from her ocean palace to be accompanied by Chameleon, she could not believe her eyes. Chameleon was wearing the same outfit as she. Mermaid had to change, as she could not wear the outfit of a simple messenger.

She changed to new finery made up of coral beads and magnificent jewelry. Again, Chameleon was now wearing the same outfit! Mermaid rushed back again and wore the most expensive and elaborate outfit that she owned. Now she was ready to compete but when she looked at Chameleon once more, sure enough it was dressed exactly like her.

Water spirits, such as Mermaid in the myth "The Mermaid and the Chameleon," and Mami Wata, the figure shown here, were popular among the Ibibio, Igbo, and other cultures. Mami Wata, who is often depicted as a mermaid, is frequently wreathed in snakes, as she is here. She is also capable of offering blessings or inflicting mental and physical pain on those who come near her.

At that point in time Mermaid gave up the contest and said, "If his messenger is so well dressed, how much better dressed must Chukwu be." Since then, no other god has ever challenged Chukwu.

Countless ritualistic ceremonies have been performed requiring specific dress, especially masks. Powerful energies were thought to exist, which could only be tapped through spiritual leaders. These leaders wore masks and headdresses to act as sacred intermediaries between humans and gods, who had the power to harm or protect. The central function of the headdress was to represent and invoke the deities. By manifesting the spirit in the human world a mask might protect people from evil forces or give a warrior power over his enemies.

4 THE SPIRIT WORLD

Africans drew spiritual inspiration for their myths from their surroundings, including animals, mountains, rivers, and food. In addition, Africans worshipped their own deities as well as the gods from Christianity and Islam. Many people in the tropical and southern regions of Africa accepted the idea of a "high god," or a sky god, often associated with thunder and lightning. Africans believed that spirits controlled nature and could interfere in daily life. People made offerings to these spirits to keep them happy. They also believed that their dead relatives could talk to the spirits to assist with their living relatives' protection and happiness. There were people, especially in West Africa, called diviners. They were said to have strong links to the spirit world.

This shield is from the Masai people, a nomadic and pastoral group from eastern Africa.

These diviners informed people of what kind of offerings they had to give and what rituals the individuals or whole villages had to perform to contact the spirit world. Many of these rituals involved singing, chanting, and dancing.

Many African religions treated the forest as the house of the gods because the forest provided food, wood, and medicines from its plants. The famous Sacred Forest, near the town of Oshogbo in Nigeria, is filled with shrines to gods and goddesses. There is a shrine to the goddess of fertility, named Oshun. Women pray to her in the belief that she will honor them with many children. There is also a god named Ifa who can predict the future. People go to this shrine to ask for advice about their daily living.

The tribes see the forest as a world where spirits live. Anyone wishing to enter it has to take special precautions and to perform certain rituals. It is also the home of *ekokos*, dwarf-demons who devour human flesh and who are masters of witchcraft. It is in the forest that the sorcerer will carve a piece of wood into which he will force man's spirit to take its home. The spirit will then serve the sorcerer and travel to his master's enemies to kill them. This wooden statue is known as a fetish and is greatly feared and respected even today. The following is a myth dealing with the spirit of an ancestor.

The Bird Spirit

A father wanted to make a special meal for his family and friends, so he went into the forest and set a snare to catch an

The Sacred Forest near Oshogbo, shown here, has many shrines to various gods and goddesses. Forests and wildlife have played an important role in African mythology. Africans have a long history of living close to the land, and this relationship is expressed in the myths they tell.

animal so that he could prepare his feast of cooked meat. That night a bird got caught in the snare. The father sent his eldest son to gather the trapped animal. The son went into the forest, but as he approached the beautiful bird, it started talking to him in the boy's language. The boy quickly returned to the house without the bird.

The father could not believe that the bird could talk and sent his other son. The same thing happened, and the other son quickly came home. The father went himself to see the caught bird. Sure enough, the bird called out to him, "My son, my son, what have you come to do? What have you come to see?" He answered the bird that he was going to take it home, kill it, and serve it to family and friends. And that is just what he did.

After the bird was cooked, everyone was told the story and thought it would be best to take the cooked bird to their

This wooden bird figure, called a Sejen, is from Africa's Ivory Coast. This figure is an example of a fetish, or a carving of an animal that is believed to provide magical powers to its owner.

*ancestors' shrine outside the village. Here the village regu-
larly made offerings to their ancestors so that their spirits
would be at peace. They offered the bird to their ancestors
and then prepared to eat it. But then something miraculous
happened. Before their eyes, the cooked bird lifted its head,
opened its eyes, and sprung to life. It spread its wings and
flew up to the sky. The father asked the elders of the village
what this meant. The elders responded that the bird was the
spirit of his own father, and after he died, he had to live as
a bird in the forest. What had happened was a good thing,
as his father's spirit was now set free.*

Many Africans believed that everything in nature had a spirit,
and many believed in the notion of the spirit inhabiting human
bodies and being reincarnated after death. The spirit of a king
might come back into an animal such as a tiger or a cobra. A
mother may return as a cow to protect her child. Some spirits were
strong-willed like a lion, and some were more gentle, like the spirits of trees. Every tree had its own spirit and had the ability to kill
a man who chopped it down unless a proper ceremony was performed. Without the tree spirit's cooperation, nothing of wood could
be built. In the case of the boat, it would sink if it were made without the approval of the tree spirit.

West Africans believed that a spider was sent by the gods to
teach people his magic of weaving. Each part of a loom had
meaning. Before weaving, the weaver touched the loom and said a

prayer. The loom was believed to sing a song only the weaver could hear while weaving.

Because the cultural understanding in Africa was that everything in nature had power, such as a lion, a snake, a wild animal, and a river, they were all believed to have strong spirits.

The Boat Mascot

Every river, stream, and pool also had its own spirit. The spirit could get angry, so it was important that people say prayers and prepare offerings to the waterway. When a man drowned, for example, the Ngbandi of the Congo believed that the stretch of water where the man lost his life became the dead man's property. The dead man was able to pass ownership of the water on to his descendants. It was customary for the surviving son to visit the place and to make

The Ngbandi people, the creators of this cup from Zaire, lived on the Ubangi River, a tributary of the Congo River. The significance of the river in their lives explains the Ngbandis' unique practice of assigning a drowned man the stretch of water where he died.

offerings in his father's honor. The son would be asked to go fishing, as the spirit of his father was said to be in the area to watch over him.

To this day many African people have ritualistic prayers, give offerings, and generally respect tradition. As you can see, the spirit world is a very powerful force in African culture and mythology.

5 MYTHS ON TEACHING MORALS

Myths are not just about religion and spiritual beliefs; they also serve as educational tools and entertainment. In West Africa, for example, young children are taught what is acceptable behavior as they listen to the stories concerning mythical characters and creatures. Historical events are preserved in the African myths and are told and retold at special occasions. They serve as unique history lessons and explain how the world works.

"The Finding of Fire" is a myth in which the human being gains knowledge through quest. As a result, his actions benefit all humankind.

"The Finding of Fire"

A hunter notices a light in the woods. He seeks it out and discovers a fire that

This contemporary mask is from the Mende, who have a proud tradition of morals and initiation.

speaks to him. The fire tells the hunter he can stay but that he must feed the fire branches from nearby trees. After the hunter complies, the fire teaches him how to cook his food over the fire. After eating a cooked hare, the hunter vows never to eat raw meat again. He also feels that it is important that he take the fire back to his village, but the fire tells him "no."

The hunter continues back and forth to the fire, cooking his meat and taking it to his wife. The wife starts to gossip and tells another man about the fire. He follows her husband and watches as her husband feeds the fire branches. When the hunter has gone, the man grabs a burning branch and runs to take it back to the village. As he runs, the burning branch burns him and he then drops it to the ground.

Next, a large fire erupts, and the village is almost destroyed. Luckily, the people escape across the river. When the fire dies down and it is safe to return to their burned village, they discover that their meat has been cooked by the fire and their clay pots have hardened. The hunter makes the journey back to the original fire, which tells him that fire is only useful if it is used properly and carefully. From that day on, the hunter continued to teach the lessons learned from the talking fire.

This myth teaches people to understand the value of fire, the way it can benefit mankind, and the fact that it can also be destructive if used carelessly. In a land that is surrounded by dry grass and forests, the myth explains, fire had to be respected for its power.

Fire is such an important natural resource, not only in African society, but around the globe as well. Without fire, civilizations would thrive less quickly, with some dying out altogether. Despite all the good that fire can do for societies, it is also a destructive force. Because of fire's dual nature, it plays a versatile and educational role in African mythology. Fire is a resource that is simultaneously welcomed and feared in African cultures.

Elders in the Sande society used the following myth called "Dancing with Spirits" to instill virtues into their children as they entered into adulthood. There were celebrations that accompanied these initiations. Coming-of-age celebrations all over Africa often culminated in a dance or a ritual. Many of these dances reenacted the people's mythic origins.

One year, the Sande society was holding a masquerade. Four spirits in heaven decided to climb down a long rope to attend the festivities. The dance celebration lasted four days, and the spirits met four women. When the dance was over, the spirits had to return to the heavens.

The women pleaded to go with them. The spirits warned the women that the heavens were filled with sick people. Two of the women were convinced not to go, but the other two went with the four spirits up to the heavens.

Huwudui and Nyandebo showed their two girlfriends around. Huwudui's girlfriend refused to help relieve the suffering of the sick people, but Nyandebo's girlfriend was happy to wash their sores.

The two women soon became homesick and wanted to return to earth. Huwudui and Nyandebo reluctantly agreed to let the women go and told their chief. They were warned that they would be tested before they left. The chief set an assortment of boxes in front of them and told them each to choose a box of their liking. They were given the advice to choose an old box, not a shiny one. Huwudui's girlfriend chose the shiniest

There are themes that are common to all mythologies. One such common theme is the pursuit of knowledge and dealing with the potential dangers of knowledge. Similar in some ways to "Dancing with Spirits" is the Greek myth of Pandora. Pandora, illustrated here, possesses a jar, which she is ordered not to open. Despite the warnings, her curiosity overcomes her and she opens the jar, only to release all manner of misery and evil that it contained.

of all the boxes while Nyandebo's girlfriend, remembering what she was told, chose the oldest, most battered box.

The girls returned home to their villages with their boxes in hand. When Nyandebo's girlfriend unpacked her box, she drew out riches for the whole family and village. They had so many riches that they were able to start trading. Huwudui rushed into her home expecting her box also to be filled with riches galore. But as soon as the lid was opened by her father, out sprung a leopard that killed him. It was followed by lions and all kinds of fierce animals that ate everyone in the house and then escaped to the bush.

It is because of the greedy and selfish girlfriend that there are so many dangerous animals in the world today. On the other hand, due to the kind and wise behavior of the other woman, the Mende people became traders.

This teaching myth is reminiscent of the Greek myth of Pandora, who opened a jar that released all the evils that plague humankind. The African myth demonstrates two paths to travel: one leads to selfishness and horror, and the other leads to success and riches. It is up to the individual person to choose which path he or she would like to travel and to understand the possible ramifications of his or her choices.

In addition to myth, traditions throughout Africa were also communicated through dance, music, and art. The slaves in the New World were usually allowed to keep African musical traditions alive, although drums were sometimes banned. Plantation slaves sang as they labored under the hot sun. An individual would sing a line and the others would respond in chorus. This rhythmic pattern was found in the spirituals sung at times of worship.

Africa continues to be a land that values its musical and artistic elements. For centuries, young Africans have learned music from

Masquerade dancers, such as those shown here, have been an important part of African society, religion, and mythology throughout the centuries. There are four main roles for masqueraders: those who embody deities, those who embody ancestors, those who placate spirits, and those who entertain.

their elders. Therefore, music and dance remain largely in their place of origin. Dance in Africa is as different and varied as the people living on the continent. Dance can be seen as a mirror of culture, as it expresses a community's beliefs, values, and history.

Dance is also seen as a medium in which values and attitudes can be communicated. There are now national dance companies that perform all over Africa and the world, giving foreigners a glimpse of ancient African dances and rituals.

The myths we have learned about are kept alive by people called griots. A griot is a storyteller but also a keeper of history and an adviser in West Africa. Griots are very important to African cultures. They pass on traditions and other important information from generation to generation. Griots serve a special role in the community, as they are able to remember large amounts of history and tradition. In fact, it has been their job to hold on to as much information as they can.

Although there are still griots today, they are aging. The sad thing is that the elders, shamans, chiefs, storytellers, and witch doctors of the indigenous tribes may be a dying breed. If there is no one who has recorded or can remember their ancient mythical legends that were told around sacred fires, these treasured stories may die as well.

In Conclusion

Africa is a continent of contrasts. The media often show Africa as a land filled with poverty, war, disease, and famine, but not all Africa meets this description. Africa has many challenges to overcome, such as poverty, population growth, and damage to the environment. But Africa is rich in its resources and the diversity of its people. Africa is also filled with museums, universities, and innovative minds. Meet the modern-day Africa, a mixture of old and new.

African mythology continues to live on today, though some people say it is weakening with each successive generation. Storytellers, such as this shaman from the Dogon people of Mali, are dying and taking their knowledge of the mythology with them to the grave. Without a written record of these elders' tales and wisdom, the full account of African mythology that we benefit from today faces deterioration.

Some people believe in many gods, while others follow religions that have come to Africa more recently. Traditional masked dancers celebrate the harvest and rain, while young Africans in Western-style clothing dance in the cities' nightclubs. The rhythms of ancient drums are found in the modern music heard on CDs and digital music players. All this adds to the uniqueness of Africa.

Clyde W. Ford, writing in *The Hero with an African Face*, states:

The gods and goddesses, heavens and hells, devils and demons, heroes and heroines of myth have long since yielded to the microscopes, telescopes, and intellects of modern humans. Myths bring us into accord with the eternal mysteries of being, help us manage the inevitable passages of our lives, and give us templates for our relationship with the societies in which we live and for the relationship of these societies to the earth we share with all life. When trauma confronts us, individually or collectively, myths are a way of reestablishing harmony in the wake of chaos.

Cultures can look at their myths to bring meaning and a deeper understanding to their own lives.

GLOSSARY

barbarians People considered by others as primitive.

ceremony Set of acts based on tradition or ritual, often with religious significance.

cowrie Type of shell sometimes used as money by ancient West Africans.

culture The practices of a society that make it distinctive, such as its way of life, art, music, and religion.

dispersed Scattered in different directions.

griot A West African entertainer who tells history through performance.

heritage Something that is passed down from preceding generations.

immortality Endless life or existence.

Islam Religion based on belief in Allah as the only God, in Muhammad as his prophet, and in the Koran.

masquerade A ceremony at which everyone wears a costume and a mask.

mortality Death.

mortar A vessel in which substances are crushed.

nomads People who have no fixed home but wander from place to place.

pestle A club-shaped, handheld tool for grinding or mashing substances.

phenomena Unusual, significant occurrences.

precarious Dangerously lacking in security or stability.

primeval Belonging to the first or earliest age; original or ancient.

ritual A ceremony that is performed for cultural or spiritual recognition.

slave Someone who is owned by another person and forced to work for little or no pay.

supernatural Of or relating to existence outside the visible world.

tribe A group of families, clans, and individuals functioning as a social unit.

tsunami A very large ocean wave caused by an underwater earthquake or volcanic eruption.

vodun A lesser god of the Fon religion. Vodon, or voodoo, derives from the word *vodun*.

FOR MORE INFORMATION

Africa Action
1634 Eye Street NW #810
Washington, DC 20006
e-mail: africaaction@igc.org
Web site: http://www.africaaction.com

Mythology Webliography
Pollard Memorial Library
401 Merrimack Street
Lowell, MA, 01852
(978) 970-4120
Web site: http://www.pollardml.org/myth.html

Normal Public Library
African-American Resources
206 West College Avenue
Normal, IL 61761
(309) 452-1757
e-mail: normallibrary@normal.org
Web site: http://www.normal-library.org/R_african.shtml

Public Broadcasting Service
Wonders of the African World
1320 Braddock Place
Alexandria, VA 22314
Web site: http://www.pbs.org/wonders

South African Consulate General

333 East 38th Street 9th Floor

New York, NY 10016

(212) 213-4880

Web site: http://www.southafrica-newyork.net/consulate/arts.htm

Web Sites

Due to the changing nature of Internet links, the Rosen Publishing Group, Inc., has developed an online list of Web sites related to the subject of this book. This site is updated regularly. Please use this link to access the list:

http://www.rosenlinks.com/maw/afri

☠ FOR FURTHER READING

Allen, Tony, Fergus Fleming, and Charles Phillips. *Voices of the Ancestors, Kingdoms and Empires*. Amsterdam, Netherlands: Duncan Baird Publishers, 1999.

Anderson, David. *Origin of Life on Earth: An African Creation Myth*. Mt. Airy, MD: Sights Productions, 1991.

Holmes, Timothy. *Zambia* (Cultures of the World). New York, NY: Marshall Cavendish, 1998.

Larungu, Rute. *Myths and Legends from Ghana for African-American Cultures*. Mogadore, OH: Telcraft Books, 1992.

Quigley, Mary. *Ancient West African Kingdoms: Ghana, Mali,and Songhai*. Chicago, IL: Reed Educational and Professional Publishing, 2002.

Regan, Colm, and Pedar Cremin. *Africa*. Austin, TX: Raintree Steck-Vaughn Publishers, 1997.

Rosenberg, Anne. *Nigeria the Culture*. New York, NY: Crabtree Publishing Co., 2001.

Shuter, Jane. *Ancient West African Kingdoms*. Chicago, IL: Reed Educational and Professional Publishing, 2003.

BIBLIOGRAPHY

Campbell, Joseph. *The Masks of God: Creative Mythology*. London, England: Penguin Books, 1968.

Campbell, Joseph. *The Masks of God: Occidental Mythology*. London, England: Penguin Books, 1964.

Campbell, Joseph. *The Masks of God: Oriental Mythology*. London, England: Penguin Books, 1962.

Feldman, Reynolds, and Cynthia Voelke. *A World Treasury of Folk Wisdom*. San Francisco, CA: Harper Collins, 1992.

Ford, Clyde. *The Hero with an African Face*. New York, NY: Bantam Books,1999.

Giles, Bridget. *Myths of West Africa*. Austin, TX: Raintree Steck-Vaughn Publishers, 2002.

Knappert, Jan. *Kings, Gods and Spirits from African Mythology*. New York, NY: Schocken Books, 1986.

Leslau, Charlotte, and Wolf Leslau. *African Proverbs*. Mount Vernon, NY: Peter Pauper Press, 1962.

Mbitu, Ngangur, and Ranchor Prime. *Essential African Mythology*. London, England: Thorsons, 1997.

Parrinder, Geoffrey. *African Mythology*. London, England: The Hamlyn Publishing Group Ltd., 1967.

Scheub, Harold. *A Dictionary of African Mythology*. New York, NY: Oxford University Press, 2000.

Zahan, Dominique. *The Religion, Spirituality, and Thought of Traditional Africa*. Chicago, IL: University of Chicago Press, 1979.

 INDEX

About the Author
Drs. Sandra and Owen Giddens make their home in Toronto, Canada. Sandra Giddens is a special education consultant at the Toronto District School Board. Owen Giddens is a psychological consultant at the Toronto District School Board, as well as director of a counseling agency. They have traveled extensively studying myths from around the world.

Photo Credits
Cover, p. 37 Courtesy of the Michael C. Carlos Museum of Emory University; p. 5 © AP/Wide World Photos; p. 7 Courtesy of the Division of Anthropology, American Museum of Natural History [90.1/6067]; p. 8 (left) © Royalty Free/Corbis; pp. 8–9 © Joy Tessman/National Geographic/Getty Images; p. 10 Giraudon/Art Resource, NY; p. 12 © Jim Zuckerman/Corbis; p. 14 Art Resource, NY; p. 17 Museum fur Volkerkunde, Vienna, Austria/Bridgeman Art Library; p. 19 © Charles & Josette Lenars/Corbis; p. 20 Courtesy of the Division of Anthropology, American Museum of Natural History [90.1/8429 AB]; p. 21 © Lord and Lady Oxmantown Collection, Art & Artifacts Division, Schomburg Center for Research in Black Culture, The New York Public Library, Astor, Lenox and Tilden Foundations; pp. 23, 41 © David Wall/Alamy; p. 24 (inset) © Hamill Gallery, Boston, MA; pp. 24–25 © Giacomo Pirozzi/Panos Pictures; p. 27 Werner Foreman/Art Resource, NY; p. 30 Courtesy of the Division of Anthropology, American Museum of Natural History [90.2/7573]; pp. 32, 44 © Werner Forman/Corbis; p. 33 The Art Archive/Antenna Gallery Dakar Senegal/Dagli Orti; p. 35 Mary Evans/Harry Rountree; p. 39 © Bonhams London, UK/Bridgeman Art Library; pp. 42, 46 © Heini Schneebeli/Bridgeman Art Library; p. 52 © Michael Graham-Stewart/Bridgeman Art Library; p. 48 © Todd Pearson/Getty Images; p. 50 © Bettman/Corbis; p. 54 © Bryan & Cherry Alexander Photography/Alamy.

Designer: Thomas Forget; Editor: Nicholas Croce
Photo Researcher: Nicole DiMella